W9-ANQ-379

Giftbooks in this "Words for Life" series:

Words on Hope	Words on Joy
Words on Courage	Words on Kindness
Words of Wisdom	Words on Love and Caring
Words on Compassion	Words on Solitude and Silence
Words on Beauty	Words on Strength and Perseverance
Words on Calm	Words on a Simple Life

Published simultaneously in 1998 by Exley Publications Ltd. in
Great Britain, and Exley Publications LLC in the USA.
Copyright © Helen Exley 1998
The moral right of the author has been asserted.

12 11 10 9 8 7 6 5 4 3 2 1

Edited and pictures selected by Helen Exley
ISBN 1-86187-041-8

Printed in Hungary.

**Exley Publications Ltd, 16 Chalk Hill, Watford,
Herts WD1 4BN, UK.
Exley Publications LLC, 232 Madison Avenue,
Suite 1206, NY 10016, USA.**

Words on Compassion

A HELEN EXLEY
GIFTBOOK

NEW YORK • WATFORD, UK

*We must not only give
what we have;
we must also give
what we are.*

DESIRE-JOSEPH MERCIER
(1851-1926)

*COMPASSION — LITERALLY
"SUFFERING WITH" — IS
BORN OUT OF FEELING
THE RAWNESS OF THE
HEART, WHICH ALSO MAKES
US MORE SENSITIVE
TO OTHERS.*

JOHN WELWOOD

Spiritual energy brings compassion into the real world. With compassion, we see benevolently our own human condition and the condition of our fellow human beings. We drop prejudice. We withhold judgement.

CHRISTINA BALDWIN,
FROM "LIFE'S COMPANION, JOURNAL
WRITING AS A SPIRITUAL QUEST"

I HAVE FOUND THAT THERE IS A TREMENDOUS JOY IN GIVING. IT IS A VERY IMPORTANT PART OF THE JOY OF LIVING.

WILLIAM BLACK

Happiness is if you give it away.

CHRISTOPHER HOARE, AGE 11

She gives most who gives with joy.

MOTHER TERESA
(1910-1997)

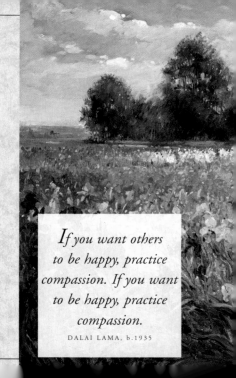

*If you want others
to be happy, practice
compassion. If you want
to be happy, practice
compassion.*

DALAI LAMA, b.1935

What is the best gift you ever received? Better still, what is the best gift you ever gave? Perhaps you will recall that in each instance, the best gift was one that was tied with the heartstrings of the giver, one that included a part of self.

WANDA FULTON

Compassion acts like rain upon dry ground

DR. MAYA V. PATEL, b. 1943

Compassion is the deepest wellspring of the human spirit, running under the hills of everyday life, feeding the rivers and oceans of all the other virtues.

ARMAND EISEN

*Compassion is the basis of
all morality*

ARTHUR SCHOPENHAUER
(1788-1860)

Part of her gift in bringing comfort to those in anguish lay in this sensitive awareness of when silence is best. She was not a voluble sympathiser, quite the reverse. At some point during an outpouring of grief, she would stretch out a hand or both hands and touch the person on the arm or face.

W.F. DEEDES,
ON A TRIP TO BOSNIA
WITH DIANA,
PRINCESS OF WALES

*The happiness of life is made
up of minute fractions -
the little, soon-forgotten charities
of a kiss, a smile, a kind look,
a heartfelt compliment
in the disguise of a playful
raillery, and the countless
other infinitesimals of
pleasant thought and feeling.*

SAMUEL TAYLOR COLERIDGE
(1772-1834)

*No one
is useless
in this world
who lightens
the burden
of it
for anyone else.*

CHARLES DICKENS

(1812-1870)

*All the beautiful
sentiments
in the world
weigh less
than a single lovely
action.*

JAMES RUSSELL LOWELL
(1819-1891)

*After the verb
"to love", "to help"
is the most beautiful
verb in the world.*

BARONESS
BERTHA VON SUTTNER

THE LOVE
WE GIVE AWAY
IS THE ONLY LOVE
WE KEEP.

ELBERT HUBBARD

It's not how much we give,
but how much love
we put in the doing –
that's compassion in action.

MOTHER TERESA
(1910-1997)

THE GOLDEN LADDER
OF GIVING

To give reluctantly.

*To give cheerfully, but not in
proportion to the need.*

*To give cheerfully, and proportionately,
but not until solicited.*

*To give cheerfully, proportionately,
and unsolicited, but to put the gift into
the poor person's hand, thus creating
shame.*

*To give in such a way that the
distressed may know their benefactors,
without being known to them.*

*To know the objects of our bounty, but
remain unknown to them.*

To give so that the benefactor may not know those who have been relieved, and they shall not know him.

To prevent poverty by teaching a trade, setting a person up in business, or in some other way preventing the need of charity. This is the highest step in charity's golden ladder.

MAIMONIDES

(12TH CENTURY JEWISH SCHOLAR)

The most I can do for my friend is simply to be his friend. I have no wealth to bestow on him. If he knows that I am happy in loving him, he will want no other reward.

HENRY DAVID THOREAU
(1817-1862)

Her little girl was late arriving home from school so the mother began to scold her daughter, but stopped and asked,

"Why are you so late?"

"I had to help another girl. She was in trouble," replied the daughter.

"What did you do to help her?"

"Oh, I sat down and helped her cry."

AUTHOR UNKNOWN

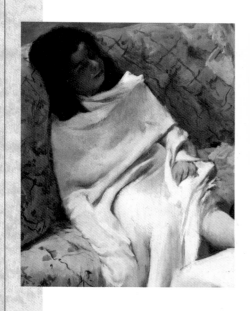

THOSE WHO ARE UNHAPPY HAVE NO NEED FOR ANYTHING IN THIS WORLD BUT PEOPLE CAPABLE OF GIVING THEM THEIR ATTENTION.

SIMONE WEIL
(1909-1943)

Most people don't just want soup, they want contact where they are appreciated, loved, feel wanted and find some peace in their hearts. It's the personal touch which matters.

SISTER DOLORES

WE KNOW THAT GOD'S ARITHMETIC IS SOMEWHAT ODD. WHEN YOU SUBTRACT BY GIVING AWAY, YOU GET MORE. WHEN YOU SEEK TO HOARD, SOMEHOW YOU LOSE OUT.

ARCHBISHOP DESMOND TUTU,
b.1931

You have not lived a perfect day, even though you have earned your money, unless you have done something for someone who will never be able to repay you.

RUTH SMELTZER

*For Diana, Princess of Wales,
there were no strangers.
All humanity was her friend.
The bereaved, the dying, the
sick and homeless,
the outcasts and the despised
– these were her close friends.
She treated them as allies in*

*the veil of tears they shared
with her.
Often she had nothing to give
but her love and sympathy.
But that was a great deal to
those who received it and the
hundreds of millions who
witnessed, on television and
in photographs, the sincerity
of the giving and the gentle
joy of the response.*

PAUL JOHNSON, IN THE "DAILY MAIL",
SEPTEMBER 1ST, 1997

A *lifetime of little*
kindnesses may well
outweigh one of great
achievement.

PAM BROWN, b.1928

THE BEST PORTION OF

A GOOD MAN'S LIFE;

HIS LITTLE NAMELESS,

UNREMEMBERED ACTS

OF KINDNESS AND

OF LOVE.

WILLIAM WORDSWORTH
(1770-1850)

Familiar acts are beautiful
through love.

PERCY BYSSHE SHELLEY
(1792-1822)

In a little Indiana town, there was a 15-year-old boy with a brain tumor. He was undergoing radiation and chemotherapy treatments. As a result of those treatments, he had lost all of his hair. I don't know about you, but I remember how I would have felt about that at his age –
I would have been mortified!
This young man's classmates spontaneously came to the rescue: all the boys in his grade asked their mothers if they could shave their heads so that Brian wouldn't be the only bald boy in the high

school. There, in the local
newspaper, was a photograph of a
mother shaving off all of her son's
hair with the family looking on

approvingly. And in the
background, a group of similarly
bald young men.

HANOCH MCCARTY

*Empathy is your pain
in my heart.*

AUTHOR UNKNOWN

A little thought will show you how vastly your own happiness depends on the way other people bear themselves toward you. The looks and tones at your breakfast table, the conduct of your fellow workers or employers, the faithful or unreliable men you deal with, what people say to you on the street, the letters you get, the friends or foes you meet - these things make up very much of the pleasure or misery of your day. Turn the idea around, and remember that just so much are

*you adding to the pleasure or the
misery of other people's days....
Whether each day of your life*

*shall give happiness or
suffering rests with yourself.*

GEORGE S. MERRIAM

THE POOR NEED MORE THAN GIFTS. THEY NEED TO BE NEEDED.

PAM BROWN, b.1928

Often with the poorest people you cannot completely alleviate their problem but by being with them, by being for them, whatever you can do for them makes a difference.

BROTHER GEOFF,
THE MISSIONARIES
OF CHARITY BROTHERS

We can cure physical
diseases with medicine
but the only cure for
loneliness, despair
and hopelessness is
love. There are many
in the world who are
dying for a piece of
bread but there are
many more dying for
a little love.

MOTHER TERESA
(1910-1997)

Benevolence doesn't consist in those who are prosperous pitying and helping those who are not.

Benevolence consists in fellow feeling that puts you upon actually the same level with the fellow who suffers.

WOODROW WILSON
(1856-1924)

WHEN I give
I give myself.

WALT WHITMAN
(1819-1891)

*Compassion is being in tune
with oneself, the other
person and the whole world.
It is goodness at its most
intuitive and
unreflective. It is a harmony
which opens itself and
permits the flowing out of
love towards others without
asking any reward.*

DAVID BRANDON

There are so many sorrows in today's world! These sorrows are due to hunger, to dislodging, to all kinds of illnesses. I am convinced that the greatest of all sorrows is to feel alone, to feel unwanted, deprived of all affection. It consists in not having anyone, in having gotten to the point of forgetting what human contact is, what human love is, what it means to be wanted, to be loved, to have a family.... May we all be

instruments of peace, of love, and of compassion.

MOTHER TERESA (1910-1997)

In our attitudinal healing workshops, we often ask, "If this is your last day on earth, how would you want to be described?" Ninety-nine percent of the time, the reply is, "I did my best to love other people and to make a difference by being caring and compassionate." And yet, when most of us look at our day-to-day lives and our style of loving, it wouldn't look that way at all.

R. CARLSON AND B.SHIELD,
FROM "HANDBOOK FOR THE SOUL"

THE SIMPLE THINGS
ARE OFTEN BEST:
A SIMPLE,
HELPING HAND,
A KINDLY THOUGHT,
THE SIMPLE PHRASE,
"OF COURSE I UNDERSTAND."

ANNE KREER

*If someone listens, or stretches
out a hand, or whispers a kind
word of encouragement, or
attempts to understand a lonely
person, extraordinary things
begin to happen.*

LORETTA GIRZARTIS

A look filled with understanding, an accepting smile, a loving word, a meal shared in warmth and awareness are the things which create happiness in the present moment. By nourishing awareness in the present moment, you can avoid causing suffering to yourself and those around you. The way you look at others, your smile, and your small acts of caring can create happiness.

THICH NHAT HANH

Love is all we
have, the only way
that each can help
the other.

EURIPIDES

I had found a kind of serenity,
a new maturity…. I didn't feel
better or stronger than anyone else
but it seemed no longer important
whether everyone loved me or not —
more important now was for me to
love them. Feeling that way turns
your whole life around;
living becomes the act of giving.

BEVERLY SILLS

IF WE DON'T
HELP EACH OTHER,
WHO WILL?

BARBARA MANDRELL

MAY NO ONE EVER
COME TO SEE YOU
WITHOUT GOING AWAY
BETTER AND HAPPIER.
EVERYONE SHOULD SEE
KINDNESS IN YOUR FACE,
IN YOUR EYES,
IN YOUR SMILE.

MOTHER TERESA
(1910-1997)

There is no need to go searching for a remedy for the evils of the time. The remedy already exists — it is the gift of one's self to those who have fallen so low that even hope fails them.

RENÉ BAZIN
(1853-1932)

THE OPPORTUNITY
TO PRACTISE BROTHERHOOD
PRESENTS ITSELF EVERY TIME
YOU MEET A HUMAN BEING.

JANE WYMAN

I expect to pass through life but once.
If therefore, there be any kindness
I can show, or any good thing
I can do to any fellow being,
let me do it now, and not defer
or neglect it,
as I shall not pass this way again.

WILLIAM PENN
(1644-1718)

What do we live for,
*if it is not to make life less
difficult for each other?*

GEORGE ELIOT
(MARY ANN EVANS)
(1819-1880)

Acknowledgements: The publishers are grateful for permission to reproduce copyright material. Whilst every reasonable effort has been made to trace copyright holders, the publishers would be pleased to hear from any not here acknowledged. W.F. DEEDES: From "The Princess of Sorrows" from *The Daily Telegraph*, September 1997. Reprinted with permission. THICH NHAT HANH: From *Old Path White Clouds: Walking in the Footsteps of Buddha* (1991) by Thich Nhat Hanh. With permission from Parallax Press, California. GERALD JAMPLOSKY: From *Love is The Answer.* PAUL JOHNSON: From "The Two Sides of Diana" from the *Daily Mail*, September 1997. HANOCH MCCARTY: From *I Don't Despair About Kids Today* by Hanoch McCarty. © 1995 Hanoch McCarty, All Rights Reserved. MOTHER TERESA: Extracts from *Heart of Joy* by Mother Teresa, first published by Servant Books © 1995 Jose Luis Gonzalez-Balado. From *A Simple Path* by Mother Teresa published by Rider Books, an imprint of Random House UK Ltd. From *A Life for God* by Mother Teresa © 1995 Servant Books.

Picture credits: Exley Publications would like to thank the following organizations and individuals for permission to reproduce their pictures. Whilst every reasonable effort has been made to trace the copyright holders, the publishers would be pleased to hear from any not here acknowledged. Art Resource (AR), Artworks, Bridgeman Art Library (BAL), Edimedia (EDM), Fine Art Photographic Library (FAP), Giraudon, Scala, SuperStock (SS).

Cover and Title Page: © 1998 Patrick William Adam, *Flower Border*, BAL; pages 6/7: Pissaro, *Landscape at Fragay*, Giraudon; page 9: Léon J. F. Bonnat, *Detail*